THE AGE OF BLISS

UTHMAN رضي الله عنه
IBN AFFAN

RUHİ DEMİREL

NEW JERSEY • LONDON • FRANKFURT • CAIRO • JAKARTA

TUGHRA
BOOKS

Translated by Asiye Gülen
Edited by Clare Duman

Published by Tughra Books
335 Clifton Ave., Clifton,
NJ, 07011, USA

www.tughrabooks.com

Library of Congress Cataloging-in-Publication Data Available

ISBN: 978-1-59784-373-7

TABLE OF CONTENTS

Uthman ibn Affan ﷺ

A Dream
Come True

*a*long caravan with fully loaded camels was making its way through the desert from Damascus. The weary travellers were anxious about being attacked by bandits; the trade routes were renowned for highwaymen who made their living from murdering people and robbing caravans.

"Stop!" The chief of the caravan brought the travellers to a halt. "The camels are tired. We'll rest here for a while and continue later." After quickly unloading the camels, some people slept while others kept watch and guarded the caravan.

A thirty-four year old man, thickly bearded and with bushy hair, scanned the caravan and the surrounding area. Always smiling, even when he was alone, Uthman, may Allah be pleased with him, saw that the guards were all awake and watchful. Allowing his eyes to gently close, he drifted into sleep and began dreaming.

"Everyone, wake up!" The man in his dream was walking through the caravan shouting loudly, "Ahmad has declared his Prophethood in Mecca!"

Filled with excitement, Uthman awoke and looked around him, blinking from the harsh glare of the sun. Nothing unusual was happening. The camels were chewing the cud, the guards were watching over the caravan and everyone else was sleeping. Uthman pondered over his dream. Who was Ahmad? What could it mean?

A short while later, the travellers were woken up, the camels were repacked with goods and the caravan continued on its way. Finally, after a long and tiring journey, the caravan arrived in Mecca. The goods they had brought with them from Damascus were displayed in the bazaar and quickly sold.

With his business finished, Uthman wandered through the city, deep in thought. He visited the Ka'ba and circumambulated it as was the tradition. He stopped and absentmindedly watched the other people who were there, praying in front of the many idols laid out in the courtyard.

Turning his back to leave, he felt a hand on his shoulder. Surfacing from his daydream he saw that it was his close friend, Abu Bakr, may Allah be pleased with him. Smiling, Uthman greeted his dear friend.

Abu Bakr had recently accepted Islam and frequently visited his close friends to tell them about this new religion. After catching up, the friends started talking about the idols and how a person can discover true serenity within oneself. Abu Bakr took the opportunity to tell Uthman about the noble Prophet and suggested they go to meet him.

Uthman was well acquainted with the blessed Prophet and referred to him by his nickname, Al-Amin, (the Trustworthy). Just like everyone in Mecca, he loved and respected him. The noble Prophet was in fact his cousin; his mother was the twin sister of Abdullah, the father of Messenger of Allah, peace and blessings be upon him.

Happily agreeing, the two friends went to visit the blessed Prophet who greeted them smiling. He enquired as to their well-being, then began to speak with his crystal clear voice, addressing Uthman, "O Uthman, you can have faith in the Paradise that Allah promises. I've been sent to guide you and all people on this path; the path which acknowledges there is no deity but Allah."

When he heard the noble Prophet speak, Uthman felt a strong feeling in his heart. Listening to his words, he felt a mounting excitement. Each of the words that the Messenger of Allah spoke filled him with exhilaration and the understanding that he had found the truth. The blessed Prophet explained to Uthman about the goodness and beauty of Islam, then looking deeply into Uthman's eyes, he recited the verse:

> And in the heaven there is your provision, and what you are promised. Then, by the Lord of the heaven and the earth, this (promise) is as much (a fact conveyed to you) as that you speak. (Adh-Dhariyat 51:22–23).

Uthman felt his hair stand on end and in that moment he was convinced to accept Islam. Reciting the *shahada*, the declaration of faith, he felt reborn, as if his heart had wings. It was with a feeling of immense lightness that he left the noble Prophet that day.

Torture

Almost bursting with anger, Hakam was looking for his nephew, Uthman. When he finally found him he managed to suppress his fury and said, "O nephew, I heard you accepted Muhammad's religion. Is this true?"

When Uthman confirmed the rumor, Hakam was dumbstruck. After a few seconds he forced a smile and said, "Now Uthman, you know I love you very much, you are like a son to me. But, what you have done makes me very sad. What shall I say to our relatives? How can I face them after this?"

Speaking softly and kindly to Uthman, Hakam tried to persuade him back to the old religion. How-

ever, confident in his newfound belief, Uthman could not be shaken. No matter how hard he tried, Hakam couldn't get him to change his mind. Finally bursting, he shouted, "O nephew, I am against you becoming Muslim. You refuse to return to our religion, but I know how I can make you."

Uthman loved his uncle very much but even so, he stayed firm in his decision and said to his uncle, "I swear to Allah that I will never again practice the religion of my forefathers."

Hakam was furious. His one and only nephew was defying him. This was not something he could bear. He quickly left him, returning only a few minutes later to ask him to change his mind again. When Uthman's answer remained unchanged, he grabbed him and tied him up tightly, shouting, "You left the religion of our forefathers and accepted this new religion. Either give it up, or I'll never untie the ropes!"

Uthman remained quiet while Hakam bound him. He looked into his uncle's angry face and said calmly, "By Allah! I will neither give up my religion nor leave Muhammad."

"Then I'll leave you here without food or water," Hakam screamed. Boiling with rage, he left Uthman, lying in the dust.

Uthman's mind never wavered; he would never give up Islam. Impotent with fury, Hakam began to torture him. He shut him in a small room and set fire to the outside hoping to suffocate him with the smoke. Holding out for a while, Uthman eventually fainted. Seeing his nephew unconscious brought Hakam to his senses and he brought Uthman out into the courtyard. When he came round, Hakam could see that Uthman would never give up his religion. Giving up at last, he said, "All right, do whatever you wish to do. I have said what I was going to say. From now on, you are free." With these words Hakam untied Uthman and left him there.

Pressure from His Mother

eturning home full of happiness after a meeting with the noble Prophet, Uthman was greeted by his mother, Arwa, who was at the door waiting for him.

"Uthman."

Uthman knew what his mother was going to say. Like his uncle, Hakam, she too wished him to return to his old religion. Taking a deep breath and summoning all her motherly authority, Arwa said, "If you do not return to the religion of your forefathers, I swear to you I won't live here anymore with you. Not under the same roof. Nor will I eat the food you bring or wear the clothes you buy for me."

Uthman loved his mother dearly and would never willingly upset her, but, even for her he could not forsake Allah or give up his religion.

Seeing the firm expression on his face, Awra understood that Uthman would never turn his back on his new faith. However, forcing the matter a little more, she continued, "I'm going to live with my sister and I won't return until you give up this new religion."

A woman of her word, Awra did what she said. Packing her bags, she left for her sister's house, thinking about her son on her journey. The sad glances he had shot in her direction as she left gave her some hope. He was a compassionate boy who didn't wish to hurt anyone. She had little doubt that in a few days he would come to her saying, "Don't be sad mother, I will return to the religion of my forefathers, just come home."

Awra couldn't have been more wrong. Uthman was upset that his mother had left their home but he was more upset that she refused to understand and accept this beautiful new religion. He wished she would come and say to him, "O son, you are right to accept Islam. Take me to Muhammad so that I too may accept this religion."

The months passed and Awra frequently asked people about her son, wondering whether he had yet changed his mind about his religion. Every day she sat at the window, waiting for him to arrive, but Uthman never came. His faith was so strong, nothing would make him renounce it, even if the whole world was against him. At last, Awra understood this and, accepting that her insistence would bring no benefit to anyone, she finally returned home.

Emigration

Life was full of difficulties for the Muslims in Mecca. Even simple tasks like going to the bazaar were full of danger. They couldn't be sure they would return home safely. The polytheists looked at them with disgust and hatred, spreading malicious rumors about them and making evil plans to harm them. In fact, this only served to deepen the Muslims' faith and strengthen their resolve.

The noble Prophet was well aware of the hardships the Muslims were enduring and constantly prayed for them. He encouraged them to be patient and endure their situation but each day, the torture increased.

One night, with the permission of the blessed Prophet, a few people left Mecca and began to travel across the desert. They were going to Abyssinia to seek refuge with the king who was said to be wise and compassionate. The Messenger of Allah entrusted the migrants to the care of Uthman. A wealthy tradesman, Uthman had given up everything for Allah and the noble Prophet. Along with his wife, Ruqayyah, may Allah be pleased with her, daughter of the blessed Prophet, he was leading the group on foot. Later the Messenger of Allah, peace and blessings be upon him, would say about Uthman, "Uthman is the next man after the Prophet Lut, emigrating with his family."

Arriving safely in Abyssinia, the group was warmly welcomed by the king who granted them refuge and freedom. Meanwhile, Ruqayyah gave birth to a healthy baby boy, delighting Uthman who named his son, Abdullah, may Allah be pleased with him. Little Abdullah was a joy for the family who were constantly homesick for their beloved city.

The emigrants were always anxious to hear good news from Mecca. They spent many hours speaking fondly of Mecca and, at long last, good news came.

Hugging each other and weeping tears of joy, the emigrants could hardly believe what they had heard.

"Did you hear? Everyone in Mecca has become Muslim."

"Thanks be to Allah! Even Abu Jahl became Muslim."

"What wonderful news. There is nothing to stop us now from returning to Mecca!"

"What are we waiting for? Let's pack our bags and go home, back to Mecca."

The emigrants packed their belongings and set out into the desert heading for Mecca, the smiles on their faces replacing the tears they had arrived with when last completing that long journey.

When they reached the city gates, they realized there had been a big mistake. Nothing had changed. The news that everyone had become Muslim was false. Even that hard-hearted polytheist, Abu Jahl, was the same as before.

Having come all this way, Uthman didn't want to return to Abyssinia to live in exile. He missed the beloved Prophet and his home city too much. Appealing to a powerful friend, he asked for protection for him and the other emigrants against the polytheists. Accepting Uthman's request, the man said to the Meccan's, "Uthman and his companions are under my protection. None of you may touch them as long as I live!"

With this promise, Uthman and his companions finally entered Mecca. Not long after, the noble Prophet gave permission for the Muslims to emigrate to Medina and Uthman was among those who migrated. On arriving in Medina, Uthman and his family were hosted by one of the Medinan Helpers until Uthman had built them a home.

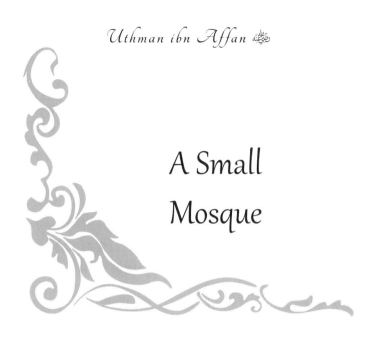

A Small
Mosque

rriving in Medina, the blessed Prophet built a mosque for the Muslims to pray in. The land for the mosque was purchased by Abu Bakr and the mosque was big enough for all the Muslims living in Medina.

Within a short time, the number of Muslims had grown so large that the mosque was no longer big enough to house them all for the prayers. One day, looking at the mosque, the noble Prophet announced, "Whoever can make this mosque bigger will be rewarded by Allah with Paradise."

Uthman quickly stood up and said, "Please, let me make our mosque big enough for everyone who wants to worship here."

He bought the land surrounding the mosque and enlarged the building making it forty times bigger. The noble Prophet was pleased with the new space and prayed for Uthman. Shortly after the completion of the mosque, the noble Prophet received this revelation from the chapter At-Tawbah (The Repentance):

> Only he will maintain Allah's houses of worship (using them for the purposes for which they are built) who believes in Allah and the Last Day, and establishes the Prescribed Prayer, and pays the Prescribed Purifying Alms, and stands in awe of none but Allah. It is hoped that such (illustrious) persons will be among the ones guided to achieve their expectations (especially in the Hereafter). (At-Tawbah 9:18).

Uthman ibn Affan ﷺ

The Well
Called Ruma

M edina days were long and hot. Many of the city's inhabitants worked in the vineyards and orchards. In their breaks they would run to get the water pitchers, reinvigorated by drinking after sweating in the heat. But the bitter, harsh tasting water in Medina was only enjoyed by the desperately thirsty.

Medina's only fresh water well was located outside the city and was owned by a Jewish merchant who had a reputation for being unfair in the way he sold the water. People had to pay him for the water before he would unlock the lid to let them fill their pitchers. Many of the poor were unable to afford his prices and had no choice but to drink the city's bitter water. Sometimes poor people would bring their pitchers to him but he would ask, "Do you have any money?"

"No I haven't. But I can bring you money later when I have enough to pay you."

Then, shaking his head the Jewish man would reply, "No. The well water is decreasing every day and nowadays there is also no rain. If I were to give everybody free water how I would ensure that I had some for myself? Come later when you have money to pay for it."

People had begun to be disturbed by the man's behavior and the topic reached the ears of the noble Prophet. As the people explained the situation to him, the blessed Prophet was saddened about their lack of access to fresh water and suggested, "Whoever is willing to buy the well will be rewarded by Allah in Paradise."

Uthman went to the Jewish man and offered to buy the well. When the man refused, Uthman offered a higher price which the man agreed to with one condition. He explained in a pleasant way, "All right. I will sell you half of the water. That's what I'm willing to give you. You can sell your half of the water and earn money and I can sell the other half and earn money as well."

Uthman agreed to these terms and he and the Jewish man took it in turns to use the well, one using it one day and the other using it the next day. When it was Uthman's day, he gave away the water free of charge while the merchant continued to charge the same price when it was his turn.

All the people were happy with this arrangement. Even the other Jewish people who had previously paid for their water were happy because they visited the well on Uthman's days and received their water free of charge.

A short while later, the Jewish man began to regret the arrangement. Nobody visited the well on his days. While he was waiting for customers one day, he began to talk to himself, "Look at this. On my days, not a man or even an animal comes. The sheep used to come when they were thirsty but I don't even see a fly anymore. But, tomorrow there will be a crowd here because the water will be given away for free. How crazy I am! How could I have agreed to be a partner with Uthman when all he wants to do is give away what he has for free? I'm ruined! I can't compete with him. Maybe what I can do is sell him the other half of the well."

The man went to Medina to find Uthman. When he met him, he proposed, "I've thought about it, and I want to sell to you the other half of the well water at the same price as you paid before. What would you say to that?"

Uthman agreed and bought the other half of the well, giving the water away for free to anyone who visited it. Now the well was available every day to everyone. All the people who used it prayed for Uthman.

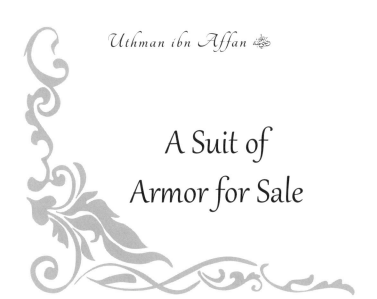

A Suit of Armor for Sale

One day, Uthman was walking through the bazaar when he heard a man's voice calling out, "I have a shield and a suit of armor for sale! Who wants to buy a shield?"

Curious, Uthman approached the stand. Several people were showing interest in the shield and two men were haggling with the trader. Recognizing the armor, Uthman asked, "Is this not Ali's armor?"

"Yes, it is," replied the trader.

"Why is he selling it?"

"He is to marry Fatima and he needs the money for the wedding."

Uthman pondered this news. Ali, may Allah be pleased with him, was a truly brave man and only he deserved such valuable armor. "How much are you selling it for," he asked.

"Four hundred dinars," said the trader.

"Give it to me and come with me to my house," Uthman said. "I'll give you the money there since I don't have it on me."

Arriving at Uthman's house, he put four hundred dinars inside the armor and paid the trader what they'd agreed. Giving the armor back to the trader he said, "Take this to Ali. Such valuable armor should only belong to him. Give him my greetings and tell him he should use the money inside for his wedding."

Uthman was indeed a charitable and good-hearted man.

Uthman ibn Affan ﷺ

A Gift

The Muslim army was poverty stricken. The hungry soldiers had neither food nor money. A piece of dry bread would have been a delicacy but even that was not forthcoming. No one complained, however; they knew the noble Prophet was in the same situation.

Within the army there were some unbelievers. These hypocrites merely pretended to be Muslim. To see the noble Prophet and his army suffering under such circumstances gladdened their hearts. Uthman, on the other hand, was very upset about the situation. One day, while he was thinking what he could do to help, he heard the blessed Prophet say,

"By Allah, before sunset Allah will give us something to eat."

Hearing this proclamation, Uthman and the other men were happy. Smiles spread over the pale, wan faces of the soldiers and they began to wait patiently for the blessing that would undoubtedly arrive.

Hours passed. Evening was approaching. The sun was beginning to set but there was still no sign of any food. The hypocrites began to gloat, whispering cynically to each other, "This time they won't get what they want. They will starve."

"You're right. Look at them. They believed the words of Muhamma, but it is useless. The sun is almost below the horizon already and no food has appeared."

Unworried and with faith in their hearts, the Muslims carried on waiting. Then somebody shouted, "Look there! Camels loaded with food are coming towards to us!"

The soldiers rose to their feet and began shouting with joy. "Allah really has sent us food. Let's go and see what has come."

Showing no interest in the throng of people around him, the man leading the camels approached the blessed Prophet directly, stopping in front of him with nine camels lined up behind. The Messenger of Allah asked him, "Where have these camels come from?"

Smiling, the man answered, "They are a gift from Uthman."

Looking joyfully at the camels, the noble Prophet opened his hands and prayed, "O Allah, give Uthman wealth. Give Uthman wealth."

The hypocrites were flummoxed by the arrival of the camels laden with food. They were sorely disappointed that the blessed Prophet had not let his followers down.

In fact, Uthman had gone to the bazaar. Buying fourteen camels along with their loads he had sent nine of them to the noble Prophet and the army. The soldiers were so thankful, they prayed for him more than they had ever prayed for anyone before.

Envy

At that time there was a poor man who was greatly saddened by his poverty. His sadness was due to the fact that he had nothing to give in the way of Allah, not because he pitied himself. He wished he were wealthy so that he could give charity for the sake of Allah and be loved by Him for his deeds. He greatly admired Uthman and his charitable deeds and would often say, "I wish I could be like Uthman."

One day, while waiting in front of the mosque, the man saw Uthman and said to him, "How lucky you are. You are rich and can give charity to poor people. You can buy slaves and give them their freedom. You can go to the Ka'ba for pilgrimage anytime you wish."

Looking at the man compassionately, Uthman replied, "Do you envy me?"

The man nodded, "Yes, I envy you very much," he said. "You are able to do so many good deeds for the sake of Allah."

Smiling, Uthman answered, "Don't be sad. The little that a poor man can give is more valuable than the charity of a rich man, because the rich man gives only a part of what he has, but the poor man gives everything that he has."

Hearing these words, the man's heart was gladdened. He became content knowing that he was doing everything he could for the sake of Allah.

Justice

One day, discovering that a servant in his house had made a mistake, Uthman became angry and punished him by pulling hard on his ear. A few days later, Uthman called the servant to come next to him. Fearful of what might happen, the servant stepped forward timidly.

"Do you remember how I pulled on your ear?" Uthman asked.

Confused, the servant answered, "I remember, my lord."

"So, this is the day of justice. I'm allowing you to pull on my ear in return for what I did to you."

The servant was speechless. He looked at Uthman blankly.

"Come on son, it's time for you to mete out justice."

"But my lord..."

"But nothing. If you cannot have your justice in this life, you will make me face justice for what I did in the afterlife. So pull on my ear."

Stretching out his shaking hand, the servant held Uthman's ear with two fingers and pulled gently.

"Come on, pull harder! Think of how I pulled your ear," Uthman entreated.

This time the servant pulled on Uthman's ear as hard as Uthman had pulled on his. With this action, Uthman was freed from worrying about receiving a punishment in the afterlife for what he had done to his servant.

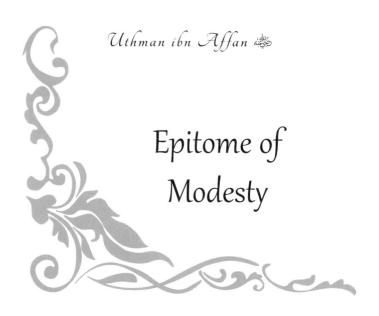

Epitome of Modesty

thman was well known for his modesty and decorum. Even the noble Prophet said about Uthman, "Of all my believers, only he is as modest in manner as I." Whether at home, or in public, Uthman displayed the same manners. Even on hot summer days he was never seen removing his clothes and pouring water on himself.

One day, this epitome of modest behavior set out to visit the blessed Prophet. The Messenger of Allah was at home with his wife, Aisha, may Allah be pleased with her. Due to the hot weather he had pulled his clothes up to his knees. Someone knocked at the door and asked permission to enter. Seeing his best friend, Abu Bakr, the noble Prophet, remained as he was and invited him in.

Soon after, Umar, may Allah be pleased with him, knocked on the door. Again, the noble Prophet remained seated and invited his friend in. The three men were deep in conversation when there was another knock at the door. Uthman had arrived and was requesting permission to enter. On hearing him, the blessed Prophet stood and lowered his clothes which had remained at his knees. The four friends had a long conversation, then the visitors left, one by one.

After they had gone, Aisha asked the noble Prophet a question which had been stuck in her mind. "O Messenger of Allah, when my father and Umar came in, you didn't lower your dress to cover your legs but when Uthman came in, you stood up and put your dress down. What was the reason for this?"

The beloved Prophet answered, "O Aisha, Allah knows that even the angels behave more modestly in front of Uthman. When this is the case, how could I not reflect his modesty and cover myself? Uthman is such a modest man that if he were to see me with me with my knees showing, he wouldn't come in. This is why I covered my legs."

Then he praised Uthman by saying, "The most modest man of all my believers is Uthman."

Glad Tidings
of Paradise

One day, the noble Prophet was visiting a near-by garden. He sat next to a well and was resting. From the garden gate, one of his Companions was watching him and waiting.

A while later, someone knocked at the garden gate. It was Uthman. He wanted to see the blessed Prophet. The Companion asked him to wait at the gate and went to let the noble Prophet know he had a visitor. The Messenger of Allah, full of joy, declared, "Let him in. Tell him to be ready for some trouble that is in store for him. Then let him know, he has the glad tidings of Paradise."

The Companion ran back to Uthman and opened the gate to him. As Uthman entered the garden he said, "O Uthman, the Messenger of Allah asked me to let you know that you will have some trouble soon."

Uthman tilted his head philosophically and said, "The one and only authority to ask for help in this case, and in every other case, is Allah."

Then the Companion said, "O Uthman, the Messenger of Allah gave you the glad tidings of Paradise."

This good news made Uthman very happy. As he walked towards the noble Prophet, he thanked Allah over and over again. When he reached him, he saw that Abu Bakr and Umar were also next to him. All of them had stretched out their bare feet into the water. Uthman joined them, rolling up his dress and dipping his feet into the cool water. As always, the four friends fell into a deep conversation.

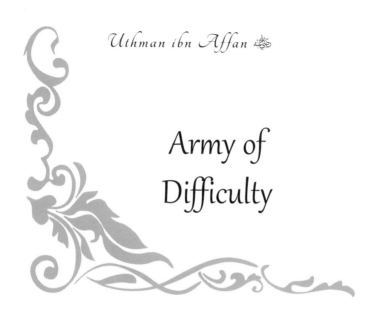

Uthman ibn Affan ﷺ

Army of Difficulty

The Muslims were preparing an army to fight the Byzantines. They named their army the "Army of Difficulty." At that time, many of the Muslims were poor. When the noble Prophet called for help to equip the army most of them had nothing to eat themselves, let alone to give away. It fell upon the rich to give as much as they could. Having arranged a meeting to discuss their needs, the beloved Prophet promised Paradise to those who helped equip the army.

"Whoever gives something to the Army of Difficulty will gain Paradise."

Rising to his feet, Uthman responded, "I will give one hundred fully loaded camels."

The noble Prophet was very pleased with this offer, but the army still required more help. Again, he called to the people for help. Uthman spoke again, "I will give another hundred camels, fully loaded," he said.

The Messenger of Allah was made even happier by this. Again, he called to the believers for help. For a third time, Uthman stood and said, "I will give another hundred camels, fully loaded."

The blessed Prophet waved his hands in admiration saying, "From now on, no one will ask Uthman to account for what he will do."

Without waiting a minute, Uthman began preparing the camels and their loads, running here and there working to put the necessary things together for the army. Seeing his efforts, the noble Prophet prayed, "O Allah, please forgive Uthman for all the sins he has done, or will do; for all the things he has done overtly or covertly; for all the things which he hides within himself or says openly."

Uthman brought hundreds of pieces of gold and presented them to the Messenger of Allah. Looking at the gold, tears rolled down the noble Prophet's cheeks. Scooping up the gold with his hands and letting it fall, he prayed, "O Allah, I am very pleased with Uthman. May You also be pleased with him."

Earthquake on the Mountain of Uhud

One day, the blessed Prophet climbed Mount Uhud with his Companions, Abu Bakr, Umar and Uthman. As they stood surveying the view of the desert below, the mountain started shaking. Stones and boulders came loose from their places and tumbled down the mountainside.

The noble Prophet looked at his friends for a moment then, turning to the mountain with a voice full of compassion he said, "Stop thy shaking, O Uhud. Standing on you are a Prophet, a holy man and two martyrs."

With these words, the mountain ceased shaking, the earthquake stopped.

Uthman and Umar knew that Abu Bakr was the holy man and that Muhammad, peace and blessings be upon him, was the Prophet. With his words, the noble Prophet had indicated that they would both die as martyrs. Until that day, everything that he had said had come true, so these words would also undoubtedly become reality.

Courier

ecca was in the hands of the polytheists. The Muslims were unable to visit the Ka'ba easily. The noble Prophet dearly wished to visit the Ka'ba and made the decision to go. He set out with 1,500 Muslims. None of the Muslims carried any weapons except their swords. Their intention was to show the Meccans that they had come in peace, not to make war. Wearing their pilgrimage clothes, they stopped within a day's walk of the city.

News of the Muslims' arrival spread through Mecca and the residents met in a state of panic. Whatever happened, they decided, the Muslims would not be allowed to enter the city. Anticipating this, the noble Prophet decided to send a courier to explain they had only come to make a pilgrimage to the Ka'ba.

The most suitable person to take the message was Uthman. In the city, Uthman had many friends and relatives and no one would harm him. With this decision made, Uthman began to walk to Mecca, the Muslims waiting at their camp with a sense of growing impatience. What would the Meccans say? Would Uthman be able to persuade them?

One of the Muslims said to the noble Prophet, "Even if they don't let us into the city, at least Uthman will be able to walk around the Ka'ba."

Turning to the believer, the blessed Prophet replied, "Without me, Uthman will never walk around the Ka'ba."

As soon as Uthman entered Mecca, he was imprisoned by the polytheists. Trying to give them the noble Prophet's message, they wouldn't listen to any of it. Insisting, Uthman said, "We will walk round the Ka'ba then return to Medina."

"We will only give permission for you to do this," the polytheists said. "The others will never be allowed in."

With a firm voice, Uthman replied, "I will never walk around the Ka'ba without the blessed Prophet."

While this was happening, the Muslims were waiting impatiently. When Uthman didn't return, they started to fear for him. Then, the rumor was spread that he had been killed, angering them and making them even more restless. The blessed Prophet could see the Muslims were restless and called them together. Speaking to each of them one by one, he put out his hand and invited them to place their hand on top of his, swearing their allegiance to him. Then, putting his hands together, the noble Prophet said, "One hand is mine and the other hand is Uthman's because Uthman strives for Allah and for me."

From this action, the Muslims understood how valuable Uthman was and how much trust the blessed Prophet had in him.

The time came to walk to Mecca. With only swords by their sides, the Muslims knew this would not be enough to save them if the Meccans wished to fight. But, none of them was afraid. When the Meccans saw their determination, they became afraid. When they understood the firm faith of the approaching Muslims, they released Uthman.

Seeing Uthman was alive and well, the Muslims became very happy. The polytheists sent a messenger to the beloved Prophet and together they worked out an agreement.

The Most
Profitable Trade

The city of Medina was in dire financial straits. No one had any food to eat or any money with which to buy some.

One day, a voice was heard calling in the street, "Uthman's caravan is coming! Uthman's caravan is coming!"

Uthman's caravans were eagerly awaited in Medina. Not only did they consist of hundreds of camels fully loaded with wheat and other food, he was also known to be very generous and would always spare a portion of the goods for the most needy.

Some of the traders in Medina, however, were not happy with this situation. They wanted to buy the goods from Uthman before he entered the city, then sell them at an inflated price. All they thought about was profit; they couldn't care less about helping their fellow man.

The traders gathered on the road outside the city, waiting for Uthman. When he arrived, they approached him saying, "O Uthman, we came here to buy your wheat."

With a firm voice, Uthman replied, "No, thank you. I am not selling the wheat."

"You aren't selling it? Why not?"

"I'm not selling the wheat, and that's it."

"We'll offer you seven times the market value." The traders were insistent.

"No, I don't wish to sell it," Uthman was determined in his answer.

"But why?"

"There is someone who will give me more than you offer me. I'm going to sell him the wheat."

However much the traders increased the price, Uthman refused to sell. He wouldn't accept any of their offers. Understanding that he wasn't to be persuaded, the traders went to complain to the caliph, Abu Bakr.

"O Abu Bakr, do you know what Uthman has done?"

"I do not, please tell me."

"Even when we insisted and offered him an excellent price he wouldn't agree to sell us his wheat. During these times of poverty can it be right what he did?

Abu Bakr thought for a while, then said, "Uthman is the son-in-law of the noble Prophet and also his Companion in Paradise; he would never do such a thing. You must have misunderstood him."

The others persisted but Abu Bakr said the same to them. Then, they all went to find Uthman. Abu Bakr explained the situation to him and asked, "O Uthman, is it true what the traders are saying?"

Smiling, Uthman looked at the people around him and said quietly, "Yes it is true. They wished to buy my wheat, but I sold it to someone else who paid me much more than they."

"Who was that?"

Uthman answered with just one word. "Allah," he said.

"What?"

"Yes, I sold all my wheat to Allah, because He gives me seven hundred times more than they could ever pay. Now I will bring the people together and give it out to them in Allah's Name."

Uthman summoned his workers and ordered them to give the wheat out to the poor and needy. But, even this was not enough for him. After doing this, he had all the camels from his caravan butchered and distributed the meat to the poor as well.

Seeing this, Abu Bakr was very happy. He kissed Uthman on the forehead and congratulated him saying, "As a matter of fact, I told the traders that they must have misunderstood you."

The next day, when Abu Bakr saw Uthman, he said to him, "O Uthman, last night I saw the Messenger of Allah in my dream. He was wearing beautiful clothes and holding a bunch of roses. I asked him 'Where are you coming from, O Allah's Messenger?' He smiled and said, 'I've just come from visiting Uthman. He performed a wonderful act of charity and Allah accepted his act.'"

Hearing this news, Uthman was very happy. Through his act of generosity he had once more earned the pleasure of the Messenger of Allah. In fact, when the noble Prophet was alive, he had always said, "Uthman is the most generous and magnanimous of all the believers."

Uthman ibn Affan ﷺ

Humility

The Messenger of Allah said, "Everyone has a close friend. My friend in Paradise is Uthman."

Even with the good news of Paradise, Uthman tried to live his life in the best way. From the night time until the morning he would read the Qur'an and worship Allah.

One night, he again rose from his bed. He left his house quietly to make his ablution for the prayers. While he was getting the water ready, someone from his household woke up and came next to him, saying, "You should have called one of the servants to come and get the water ready for you."

Uthman didn't accept this and replied, "No, the night time is their time to rest. It's not correct to deny them this right."

Everybody appreciated the unpretentious lifestyle of Uthman. Even though he was rich, he was never proud. At heart, he was a simple man and lived the same way as the other people. Even when he became caliph he continued his modest lifestyle.

Uthman didn't live in this way to impress people; his only intention was to please Allah and follow the example of the blessed Prophet.

Uthman ibn Affan ﷺ

The Generous
Old Man

One day, a child was playing with a bird close to the mosque. From his clothes it was apparent that he was from a poor family. Seeing a man sleeping, the child stopped playing with the bird and slowly drew closer to him. The man was old and had a thick beard and bushy hair. He looked so nice and peaceful the child forgot about his bird and carried on watching him, lost in thought.

The man opened his eyes and calmly observed the boy who was lost in his daydreams.

"Who are you, my boy?" asked the old man.

Coming to himself, the child quickly answered, "I'm Said's son."

The kind old man smiled and stood up. He gazed at the boy compassionately, then called to a young man who was sleeping nearby. The old man's voice wasn't loud enough to wake the youth who was in a deep sleep. He turned to the child and said, "Go and wake him up."

The child went next to the youth. Waking him, he told him that the old man wanted to see him. The youth approached the old man respectfully, listened to his whispers then ran away. The child waited full of curiosity as to what was going to happen.

A short while later, the youth returned holding a brand new dress and purse. The old man called the child next to him. With his own hands, he dressed the child and presented the purse to him saying, "There you are, my son. You may go now."

The child looked at the new clothes he was wearing and a smile spread over his face. He grinned at the old man then, running off, he went to find his father to tell him what had happened. His father was greatly surprised to hear what had taken place. Together they opened the purse and found there was some money inside. The child's father asked him to describe the old man. When he heard the description he started to smile and said, "That was the caliph of the Muslims, Uthman ibn Affan, my son."

Charity

As caliph of the Muslims, Uthman was always available for people to come and ask him for help or explain their problems to him. Some people told them their needs, while others explained the problems on their mind.

One day, someone knocked on the door. A man who seemed very sad entered the room and greeted Caliph Uthman. Uthman left what he was doing and said, "Please, my brother's son. I'm listening to you."

The man sat down and caught his breath for a moment, then started to speak, "I was praying in my garden when I heard a bird singing. It was singing so sweetly, I looked round to see where it was. It was sitting on the branch of a tree exactly opposite me. Its colors were as beautiful as its singing and I was struck with wonder as I watched it. Then, the bird flew away and, at that moment, I remembered I was supposed to be praying."

Uthman listened to the man with interest and wondered how the story would end. Without drawing it out further, the man said, "The beauty of my garden distracted me from my prayers and I am disturbed by this. To offset this sin I want to do something good. I would like to donate my garden as charity for the sake of Allah. Please take the garden and use it however you wish."

For a moment, Uthman didn't know how to respond. In fact, he hadn't been expecting something like this. Seeing the sadness on the man's face he had to accept the donation. He immediately put the garden up for sale and sold it for a good price.

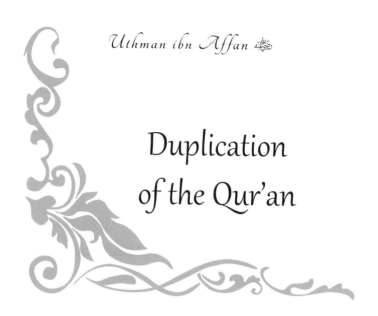

Duplication
of the Qur'an

uring the caliphate of Uthman, the Islamic army conquered many new territories, expanding the borders of the Islamic state into Europe, Africa and Asia. Not content with this, Uthman wished to conquer the islands on the seas and built up a navy to accomplish this. No land in the world should be denied the knowledge of Allah.

The success of the conquests led to the enrichment of the state. The spoils of war arrived from all over the world and were distributed to the people. At the same time, new difficulties were also encountered. The new Muslims in the conquered territories wished to learn the Qur'an. They began comparing what they had learned with each other and, finding discrepancies in the readings, they began to argue with each other, saying, "My reading is more correct than your reading; the way you are reading has mistakes in it."

Seeing the seeds of discord sprouting among the Muslim communities, one of the Companions advised Uthman, "O Caliph of the Muslims, the Muslims are arguing with each other about the Qur'an. Let's not fall into dispute about Allah's Book. We must find a solution immediately."

Uthman, who himself was devoted to the Qur'an, immediately took the matter in hand and sent a message to Hafsa, may Allah be pleased with him, "You have a copy of the Qur'an that was written in Abu Bakr's time. Please send it to me. We will make copies of it and send them out to all the Muslims."

Hafsa sent the Qur'an to Uthman who immediately commissioned the work. In a short time, six copies were made ensuring that there was no difference between any of them, not even a dot.

One copy remained in Medina and the others were sent out to the major Islamic cities. From that day onwards, everyone was able to read the original Qur'an.

Uthman ibn Affan ﷺ

The Letter

were sent out to the major Islamic cities. From that day onwards, everyone was able to read the original Qur'an.

Whenever new verses were revealed to the noble Prophet, he and his Companions immediately memorized them and had them written down. The verses were transcribed onto large date leaves, lightly colored, flat stones or leather. This work was entrusted to the best readers and writers from among the Muslims.

Marwan was one of the transcribers. The noble Prophet appointed him as "the writer of the revealed verses" and would sometimes dictate the newly revealed verses and chapters to him to write down.

One day, when he received another revelation, the blessed Prophet wished for it to be written down and called Marwan. Taking out his pen, Marwan began to transcribe everything that the blessed Prophet said. When the chapter was finished, the Messenger of Allah instructed him to name it "Al Imran."

Marwan stopped for a second, stuck on the word "Imran." He thought about his own name, "Marwan." The two names were similar to each other he thought. How about if he changed the name of the chapter to Al-Marwan instead of Al Imran? Then, the name of his family would be remembered forever. So, instead of writing down what the noble Prophet had said, he quickly wrote his own name.

The blessed Prophet immediately understood what he had done. The Qur'an is under the eternal protection of Allah. Not even the smallest word in it can be changed until the Day of Judgment. The noble Prophet spoke out and made Marwan correct the name. Then, speaking angrily he said, "It's not possible for you to stay among us anymore." Marwan was forced to leave Medina.

Marwan had committed a grave sin and, knowing that he was guilty, he accepted his punishment and left Medina.

Many years passed. The noble Prophet passed on to the eternal realm and Abu Bakr became caliph.

Marwan requested permission to return to Medina but Abu Bakr did not grant it.

Two years later, Abu Bakr died and Umar became the caliph. Again, Marwan requested permission to return and, just as Abu Bakr had before him, Umar refused. Not only did he refuse, he sent Marwan even further away from Medina.

When Uthman became the caliph, Marwan was very pleased. Uthman was known to be forgiving. Marwan visited the caliph and fell at his feet, begging and pleading to return. Seeing what he thought was Marwan's sincere regret, Uthman forgave Marwan and allowed him to live in Medina again.

Marwan became a frequent visitor to Uthman and managed to win his admiration. After a while, Uthman appointed him as his secretary.

Meanwhile, time passed. One day, a committee arrived from Egypt complaining about their governor. Uthman listened to each of them individually, then said, "All right, I will change your governor. Tell me, who do you wish me to appoint in his place?"

The committee replied, "The best person for the job is Muhammad, son of Abu Bakr."

After consulting with his advisors, Uthman agreed. He called for Marwan and dictated a letter to him, "O people of Egypt. I have dismissed your current governor and appoint in his place Muhammad, son of Abu Bakr."

Marwan was full of hatred for Abu Bakr. Not only had he prevented him from returning to Medina, because of this Umar had also refused his request and had said to him, "I would never give permission for a man to return who had not been granted permission by the Messenger of Allah or Abu Bakr." Since that day, Marwan had been waiting to take his revenge and finally, that day had come.

Secretly, Marwan wrote another letter to the governor, pretending it was on behalf of Uthman. The letter stated, "You are the governor of Egypt. Abu Bakr's son will come to you and say that you have been dismissed and that he has been appointed governor in your place. I have decided not to dismiss you, however. You must kill Muhammad and his friends."

This was a terrible plan, but Marwan was desperate for revenge and couldn't imagine that one day the truth would be revealed. The letter was written but needed the seal of the caliph to make it official.

But how could he get hold of the ring? Excited and nervous, Marwan murmured to himself as he walked to find Uthman, "The caliph never removes his ring save for when he uses the bathroom. When he goes to the toilet, he gives the ring to whoever is closest to him because the Name of Allah is written on the ring and he cannot take it into the bathroom. From now on, I will not leave the caliph's side."

Marwan arrived at the side of Uthman and, pretending to be busy with something, he began to wait. After a while, Uthman rose to use the bathroom. As Marwan was the nearest person to him, he handed him his ring and left.

For a second, Marwan didn't know what to do. He hadn't imagined it would be so easy. Not for one moment did he think about the harmful consequences of his actions for the state or for Islam. The only thing he could think of was getting revenge on Abu Bakr.

Coming to himself, he quickly sealed the letter and took it outside to a messenger saying, "This is urgent. Take it immediately to the governor of Egypt. You must be there before the committee and Muhammad otherwise everything will be in vain."

The messenger laughed sneakily, "Don't worry," he said. "I'll fly like a bird and will be in Egypt before the others."

After sending the messenger off, Marwan went back inside. Coming out of the bathroom, Uthman took his ring from Marwan and they both continued with their daily work.

Muhammad, son of Abu Bakr, may Allah be pleased with him, and the committee were on their way to Egypt. After walking for a while, they stopped on a hill to rest and from their vantage point they could see someone approaching them in a hurry. When the person came close enough to recognize them, he suddenly changed direction and ran away.

Made suspicious by this odd activity, Muhammad sent his soldiers to follow the man. A short while later, they returned to the caravan, holding him by his arms. Searching him thoroughly, they didn't find anything unusual. Then someone had the idea of searching his water bottle and it was there that they found the letter.

After reading the letter, everyone was shocked. How could it be that Uthman would write such a letter? No one wanted to believe it but the seal from his ring was there. The group packed up the caravan and set out for Medina to hold Uthman accountable for his behavior.

Seeing Muhammad return to the city so angry, the hypocrites in Medina joined him and the crowd grew very big. They went directly to Uthman and after a long argument, the truth finally came out. Everyone realized it was Marwan who had plotted to kill Muhammad.

However, the angry crowd could not be calmed. They said, "O Uthman, this is your envoy and the camel he rides is also yours. Also, the seal on the letter is yours. We know that this is the work of Marwan but it is still your responsibility. You should resign from the caliphate."

Uthman didn't accept the crowd's demands. Years earlier, the noble Prophet had warned him of what was to come saying, "O Uthman, Allah will give you a mantle to wear but the hypocrites will ask you to remove it. Don't remove it. If you do as they say, just as a camel cannot pass through the eye of a needle, you will not see Paradise."

When the discontented citizens realized that Uthman would not resign, they besieged his house.

Uthman prevented his supporters from fighting with the rebels. He didn't want to see any blood shed in the city of the beloved Prophet. Even his slaves were prepared to die fighting for him but he told them, "Whoever sets down his weapon, I'll give him his freedom."

This was a command. All the people put down their weapons.

Hearing the news of the siege, Ali called his sons to Uthman's house and ordered them, "If anyone tries to harm Uthman, take your sword and kill him. Don't let anyone into Uthman's house."

The two grandsons of the beloved Prophet unsheathed their swords and stood guard at the door of Uthman's house, ready to defend him. No one had the courage to stand against them.

A Martyr

*I*t didn't look as if the rebels would give up the siege on Uthman's house. The Medinan residents returned to their homes and waited anxiously for news. There were lots of rebels outside in the streets. In his house, Uthman was calm. He read the Qur'an as he always did.

After a while, Uthman became thirsty. Not a drop of water was left in the house and getting some from outside was impossible. The rebels wouldn't allow anyone to leave the house.

Uthman climbed onto the roof and called out to the rebels, "O Egyptians, those who are provoking you, step forward."

Two well-built men took a few steps forward. Uthman looked at them and said, "There was no other well in Medina except the Ruma well. As the Messenger of Allah wished, I bought the well with my own money. Now you are preventing me from drinking the water of this well. Do you realize this?"

At the same time, the men replied, "We take refuge in Allah, you are speaking the truth."

Uthman continued, "The mosque of our Prophet began to be too small for all the believers and the Messenger of Allah asked, 'For a reward in Paradise, who will enlarge the mosque?' I was the one who enlarged it. And, now you are not allowing me to pray in this mosque. Or is it that you didn't know about this?"

Again, the men replied together, "We take refuge in Allah, you are speaking the truth."

Taking a deep breath, Uthman continued loudly, so everyone could hear, "Say in the Name of Allah and Islam, was I the one who equipped the Army of Difficulty with my own goods?"

"Yes, you did," replied the men.

"I ask you again in the Name of Allah and Islam, one day, our Prophet, Abu Bakr, Umar and I were hiking on Mount Uhud and there was a great shaking. Large stones and boulders rolled down the mountain whereupon our Prophet said, 'O Uhud, be calm. Because standing on you there is a Prophet, a holy man and two martyrs.' Tell me, did you know this?"

Again, the men replied with the same voice, "We take refuge in Allah. This is true what you say."

Opening his hands, Uthman said, "Allah is Almighty. The Messenger of Allah named me a martyr. I swear in Allah's Name that I am a martyr."

Uthman turned and went back into his house. Some of the rebels regretted their actions. In deep sadness they immediately left the crowd. Others felt differently. Instead of giving up their siege, they continued to surround Uthman's house.

Fight?
Never!

thman was reading the Qur'an in his house, watched by his wife who had tears in her eyes. While this was happening, Abu Hurayra, may Allah be pleased with him, arrived at the house. The rebels hadn't harmed him because he was a Companion of the noble Prophet who had remained by the side of the Messenger of Allah until his death.

Abu Hurayra said to Uthman, "O caliph, now we must fight."

Uthman looked at him calmly and said, "Abu Hurayra, would it make you happy to see people die, including me?"

Without hesitating, Abu Hurayra replied, "No!"

With a painful smile, Uthman said, "Then don't fight the rebels. To kill one person is the same as killing every person."

These were the noble Prophet's words. Abu Hurayra knew them better than anyone. He thought for a moment and then turned and left.

A short while later, Abdullah ibn Zubayr, may Allah be pleased with him, came. With a firm voice he announced, "O Uthman, there are people here who want to help you. Even if they are fewer than the number of rebels, Allah will help you. Please allow us to fight."

Without even thinking, Uthman replied, "Don't you dare start something like this! If anyone wants to start shedding blood for my sake, I would remind them of their belief in Allah."

Helplessly clutching his sword, Zubayr left Uthman's house.

Next, Zayd ibn Thabit, may Allah be pleased with him, came. He had been one of the Helpers when the Muslims first migrated to Medina. Addressing Uthman he said, "O caliph, your Helpers are at the door awaiting your orders. They say, 'If the caliph of the Muslims gives permission to fight we will save him from these rebels.' What do you say?"

Uthman's reply was the same again, "Fight? Never!"

Zayd left Uthman without having been able to persuade him.

This time, a warrior named Said, may Allah be pleased with him, came to the house. With lightning in his eyes he clutched his sword cover tightly and said to Uthman, "O chief of believers."

Uthman looked at him in astonishment.

"How much longer are you going to make us wait with our hands and arms tied? These rebels are making fun of us. Some of them throw arrows, some throw stones, some of them show us their swords. At last give us your order to fight!"

Uthman addressed him softly, saying, "If I fight them I know I will win. But, by Allah, I do not want to fight. I would rather face Allah's justice. Whatever happens, soon each one of us will face judgment in Allah's presence. But to fight? I will never order this."

Said was young and spirited. He couldn't accept the cruelty the rebels were inflicting on the caliph of the Muslims. Drawing his sword, he said to Uthman, "By Allah, I will not ask anymore. I will take my sword and fight them myself."

Uthman was unable to stop him. In a flash, he ran out of the house and began fighting with the men arrayed outside. It wasn't long before he was overwhelmed and killed by the rebels.

Uthman was saddened by this event. This young warrior had yearned for quick justice. He knew that just like Said, seven hundred other warriors were waiting for his command to fight and wouldn't blink an eye about dying for their caliph. But, he could not allow this. The city of Medina should not see blood shed in its streets. He was always saying, "In my eyes, the most valuable are those who remove their hands from their weapons."

The Last Day

The rebels continued the siege of Uthman's house and began to attack it more actively. They shot arrows at the house and taunted those who wished to go inside.

The siege had lasted for forty days. On his final night, Uthman dreamed of the noble Prophet. Looking at little sad, but smiling, the Messenger of Allah looked at Uthman and asked, "O Uthman, have they surrounded your house and made you a prisoner?"

"Yes, O Messenger of Allah!"

"Uthman, have they left you without water?"

"Yes, O Messenger of Allah!"

The Messenger of Allah gave Uthman a glass of water and he drank it slowly. A cool feeling spread throughout his whole body. Then, the noble Prophet said finally, "O Uthman, do you wish for help to be rescued or do you wish to break your fast this evening with us?"

Uthman answered joyfully, "I wish to be martyred and break my fast with you, O Allah's Messenger!"

Uthman woke up. Remembering his dream he felt like his heart had wings.

A short while later, the rebels were looking for a way to enter Uthman's house. They eventually went round to the back of the house, broke down a wall and went inside.

That day, Uthman was fasting and reading the Qur'an. He behaved as if nothing was happening. The rebels surrounded and killed this great man. Uthman was eighty-two years old. Finally, after twelve years as caliph, he was reunited with Allah and His beloved Messenger.